D1109584

JUST LIKE
JESUS

Books in Series

My Time with God

God's Word in My Heart

Just Like Jesus

*I*nsomnia: a contagious disease often transmitted from babies to parents.

Shannon Fife

There is a right time for everything: A time to laugh....
Ecclesiastes 3:1,4 TLB

*F*amiliarity breeds contempt — and children.

Mark Twain

A merry heart doeth good like a medicine....
Proverbs 17:22

JUST LIKE JESUS

Paul J. Loth

Illustrated by
Daniel J. Hochstatter

THOMAS NELSON PUBLISHERS
Nashville • Atlanta • London • Vancouver

Copyright © 1995 by Educational Publishing Concepts, Inc.

All rights reserved. Written permission must be secured from the publisher to use or reproduce any part of this book, except for brief quotations in critical reviews or articles.

Published in Nashville, Tennessee, by Thomas Nelson, Inc., Publishers, and distributed in Canada by Word Communications, Ltd., Richmond, British Columbia.

The Bible version used in this publication is the Contemporary English Version. Copyright © 1991 by Thomas Nelson, Inc.

Printed in the United States of America.
ISBN 0-7852-7987-3

1 2 3 4 5 6 — 00 99 98 97 96 95

CONTENTS

An Open Letter to Children		8
Willing to Help Others	Luke 2:1–20	10
Living for God	Luke 2:21–38	12
Thinking About God	Luke 2:41–50	14
Obeying Your Parents	Luke 2:51	16
Growing Up	Luke 2:52	18
Obeying God	Matthew 3:13–17	20
Trusting in the Bible	Luke 4:1–13	22
Being Concerned About Everything	John 2:1–12	24
Loving the Church	John 2:13–22	26
Accepting Everyone	John 3:1–21	28
Being Friendly to Everyone	John 4:1–26	30
Knowing God's Word	Luke 4:16–30	32
Following God	Luke 5:1–9	34
Giving Up Things for Jesus	Luke 5:10–11	36
Pleasing God	Mark 1:40–45	38
Caring for People	Mark 2:1–12	40
Loving the Unlovely	Matthew 9:9–13	42
Helping Others First	Luke 6:6–11	44
Asking for Help	Luke 6:12–16	46
Acting on Faith	Luke 7:1–10	48
Helping Those Who Hurt	Luke 7:11–17	50
Accepting People Who Aren't Perfect	Luke 7:36–50	52

Being Part of God's Family	Luke 8:19–21	54
Being Alone	Matthew 8:18, 24	56
Trusting God	Mark 4:35–41	58
Believing in God	Luke 8:40–42, 49–56	60
Accepting Rejection	Luke 9:1–6	62
Leaning on God	Mark 6:30–44	64
Acting on Faith	Matthew 14:22–33	66
Being Clean on the Inside	Matthew 15:1–20	68
Sharing Glory with Others	Matthew 17:1–13	70
Serving Others	Mark 9:33–37	72
Having Good Friends	Matthew 18:21–35	74
Deciding Who Is Important	John 6:60–69	76
Forgiving, Not Punishing	John 8:1–11	78
Giving Glory to God	John 9:1–34	80
Taking Care of Others	John 10:1–21	82
Letting Others in on the Fun	Luke 10:1–24	84
Helping Our Enemies	Luke 10:25–37	86
Making Jesus #1	Luke 10:38–42	88
Asking God First	Luke 11:1–13	90
Deciding Who to Follow	Luke 11:14–23	92
Trusting God	Luke 12:13–34	94
Fearing No One	John 11:17–46	96
Thanking God	Luke 17:11–19	98
Not Giving Up on God	Luke 18:1–8	100
Being Humble with God	Luke 18:9–14	102
Loving Everyone	Luke 18:15–17	104
Loving God Most	Luke 18:18–30	106

Helping Others	Luke 19:1–10	108
Worshiping Jesus	John 12:1–8	110
Honoring Jesus as King	Matthew 21:1–11	112
Doing What God Wants	Luke 19:41–44	114
Praying and Believing	Mark 11:12–14, 20–26	116
Winning with Jesus	Mark 11:27–33	118
Giving All to Jesus	Mark 12:41–44	120
Helping Jesus	Mark 14:12–16	122
Letting God Pay People Back	Mark 14:17–21	124
Willing to Do Small Jobs	John 13:1–11	126
Forgetting Our Problems	Luke 22:14–23	128
Praying for Others	Luke 22:31–34	130
Preparing Through Prayer	Luke 22:39–46	132
Allowing God's Will to Be Done	John 18:1–11	134
Putting Everything in God's Hands	John 19:1–16	136
Taking Our Place	Matthew 27:11–26	138
Being Loving	Luke 23:26–38	140
Looking on the Inside	Luke 23:39–43	142
Helping Our Parents	John 19:25–27	144
Keeping Our Promises	Luke 24:1–8	146
Letting Jesus Teach Us	Luke 24:13–32	148
Helping Others Learn	John 20:24–31	150
Giving Our Friends Another Chance	John 21:15–19	152
Sending Others to Help	Acts 1:1–8	154
Telling Others About Jesus	Matthew 28:16–20	156
Helping Always	Mark 16:14–20	158

An Open Letter to Children

Who is a person you would love to meet? Do you want to be like that person? Why?

As Christians we want to be like Jesus. But first we need to get to know Him.

Just Like Jesus will help you get to know Jesus. You will learn what He is like. You will learn how to be more like Him.

It is good to spend time with Jesus. This is called devotions. Use this book for your devotions. It will help you get to know Jesus better.

Your devotion has three parts to it:

Think Start with thinking about what has happened to you and why.

Learn Next is a story about Jesus. This will help you get to know Him better.

Pray Jesus likes to hear from you, too. Prayer is your chance to talk to Him. Tell Him you love Him. Get to know Him as your friend.

Memory verses are a good way to get to know Jesus. They help keep Him in your mind for a long time. Try to memorize a verse each day.

Friends may change. But Jesus is a friend who will be with you all the time. Get to know Him a little bit each day.

Your friend and Jesus' friend,

Paul J. Loth, Ed.D.

Willing to Help Others

Luke 2:1–20

Think When was the last time you helped someone?

How did you help?

Do you like to help others?

Learn We need help. We need to be saved. God's Son, Jesus, can help us. He can be our Savior.

Jesus had to leave heaven. When Jesus left heaven, He left His glory as God's Son. He had to be a servant.

Jesus came to earth to help us. He came to save us. We can be like Jesus and help others.

Pray Thank You for helping me. Let me help others too.

He gave up everything and became a slave, when he became like one of us.

Philippians 2:7

11

Living for God

Luke 2:21–38

Think What would you like to do when you grow up? Why?

What would you like to do with your life?

Learn Jesus was a baby. His mom and dad wanted to please God. So they did what God told them to do. They took baby Jesus to the temple. They knew Jesus would want to please God too. They knew God loved Jesus.

Simeon saw Jesus. He told Mary that her child would save the world.

Your life can be special if you can live your life for God.

Pray Help me to live my life for You, Jesus.

If I live, it will be for Christ.

Philippians 1:21

13

Thinking About God

Luke 2:41–50

Think What do you like to think about most?
Why?
What do you try not to think about? Why?

Learn One day Jesus and His mom and dad took a trip. They went to Jerusalem. They stayed a few days. Then it was time to go home. But Jesus' mom and dad could not find Him. They were worried.

They looked and looked.

Jesus was in God's house, the temple. He was talking about God with the people there.

Jesus liked to think about God. Do you?

14

Pray Help me to think about You more this week.

Think about what is up there, not about what is
here on earth.

Colossians 3:2

15

Obeying Your Parents

Luke 2:51

Think Do you always obey your mom and dad? Why? Why not?

Learn Jesus grew up in Nazareth. Mary was His mom, and Joseph was His dad. Joseph was a carpenter.

Jesus knows all things. So Jesus knew more than His mom and dad! But He still obeyed them.

Jesus made God happy when He obeyed His mom and dad. Obey your mom and dad. You will make God happy too.

Pray Help me to obey my mom and dad better.

Children, you belong to the Lord,
and you do the right thing when you obey your parents.

Ephesians 6:1

17

Growing Up

Luke 2:52

Think Are you getting taller? Are you learning how to play with friends? Are you learning more about God?

Learn Jesus grew up in Nazareth. He made friends. And He learned how to play with His friends.

Jesus grew closer to God too. He went to the temple every week. And He read the Scriptures.

Growing taller is only one way to grow. Jesus grew in other ways too. How are you growing?

18

Pray Dear Jesus, help me to grow up in every way.

Jesus became wise, and his body grew strong.
God was pleased with him and so were the people.
Luke 2:52

19

Obeying God

Matthew 3:13–17

Think Do you obey your mom and dad? How do they feel when you do not obey them?
Do you obey God? How do you think God feels when you do not obey Him?

Learn John the Baptist told people to tell God they were sorry for not obeying God. He baptized people who did.

Jesus went to see John. He wanted John to baptize Him too. He had not sinned. But Jesus wanted to obey God.

So John baptized Him. And God said, "This is my own dear Son, and I am pleased with him."

Pray Dear Jesus, help me to obey. Teach me how to do the right thing.

Christ was humble. He obeyed God and even died
on a cross.
Philippians 2:8

Trusting in the Bible

Luke 4:1–13

Think Have you ever been told to do a thing that is wrong? What did you do?
What is the best way to keep yourself from doing the wrong thing?

Learn Jesus was told to do the wrong thing too. Satan wanted Jesus to disobey God. What do you think Jesus did? He quoted the Scripture to Satan! When we use the Bible, we use God's Word. Nothing is as strong as that!

Your friends may tell you to do the wrong thing. Think of a Bible verse. God will help you do the right thing.

Pray Help me to obey You all the time.

So put on all the armor that God gives . . . you will still be
standing firm.

Ephesians 6:13

23

Being Concerned About Everything

John 2:1–12

Think Do you help your friends when they need help with things? Even if the things do not seem important?

Learn Jesus went to a wedding. Jesus' mom was there. So were His friends, the disciples. But there was a problem. There was no drink left. Jesus' mom asked Him to help.

Jesus helped. He turned plain water into the best drink. We should help our friends too.

Pray Dear Jesus, I want to help people just like You did.

Our people should learn to spend their time doing something useful and worthwhile.

Titus 3:14

25

Loving the Church

John 2:13–22

Think What is your favorite place to go? Why? What do you like to do there?

Learn Jesus liked to go to God's house. But one time He was not happy there. People were selling things. That was not right. God's house is for prayer and worship.

Jesus was mad. He made a whip. Then He swung the whip. He knocked over the tables. The people selling things had to leave God's house.

God's house was special to Jesus.

Pray Dear Jesus, thank You for giving me a special house where I can learn about You.

It made me glad to hear them say, "Let's go to the house of the LORD!"

Psalm 122:1

Accepting Everyone

John 3:1–21

Think Is there a person you do not like? Who? Why do you not like that person?
Would you help that person if he or she came to you for help?

Learn Nicodemus was a Pharisee. Pharisees did not like Jesus. One night Nicodemus came to see Jesus. He had some things to ask Jesus. He made sure no one saw him. He did not want his friends to know he went to see Jesus.

Jesus was not mean to Nicodemus. He told him more about God.

Do you know someone who is mean to you? What would you do if he or she came to you for help?

Pray I want to be like You, Jesus. I want to help people, even ones who are mean to me.

Love your enemies and pray for anyone who mistreats you.

Matthew 5:44

Being Friendly to Everyone

John 4:1–26

(Think) Are you friends with everyone?
Do you talk with everyone? Why? Why not?

(Learn) Jesus was tired. He sat down to rest. Soon a woman came. She wanted to get a drink from the well. Jesus asked her for a drink too. She was shocked that He spoke to her. Jesus was a Jew. She was a Samaritan. Jews did not speak to Samaritans. But Jesus was nice to all people.

Do you love all people? Is everyone your friend? Jesus loved all people.

Pray Dear Jesus, help me to be friendly to every-one, not just my friends.

A friend is always a friend.
Proverbs 17:17

Knowing God's Word

Luke 4:16–30

Think What do you know the most about? How did you learn it? How does knowing it help you?

Learn Nazareth was Jesus' hometown. He grew up there. Then He went back as an adult. One day He went to worship God. Someone gave Him the Scripture to read. Jesus read it in the service. Then He told everyone what it meant.

Do you know the Scripture? Could you explain it like Jesus did?

Pray Teach me Your Word, Jesus. I want to be able to tell others about it, just like You did.

Open my mind and let me discover the wonders of your Law.

Psalm 119:18

33

Following God

Luke 5:1–9

Think Do you do what you are told to do?
What if someone you trusted told you to do something
that made no sense?

Learn Simon had fished all night. But he caught no fish. Jesus got into Simon's boat. "Row the boat out into the deep water," Jesus said. "Let your nets down to catch some fish."

It did not make sense to Simon. But he did what Jesus said. And he caught many fish.

Simon was glad he did what Jesus told him. One d God may tell you to do something that does not make sense. If He does, thi of Simon and his fish.

34

Pray Dear Jesus, help me to obey You, even when I do not know why.

And if they obey, they will be successful and happy from then on.
Job 36:11

35

Giving Up Things for Jesus

Luke 5:10–11

Think Have you ever had to give up one thing to get something else you wanted more?
What was it? Was it worth it?

Learn Simon loved to fish. Then he met Jesus. Jesus helped him catch a lot of fish.

Jesus wanted to help Simon fish for people. He wanted Simon to tell others about Jesus. So Simon followed Jesus. He gave up a thing he loved. But he got something better. He got Jesus.

Pray I want to follow You, too, Jesus. Help me give up those things that get in the way.

If you want to save your life, you will destroy it. But if you give up your life for me, you will find it.

Matthew 16:25

Pleasing God

Mark 1:40–45

Think Do you want to be popular?
Is it the most important thing to you?
Would you ever give up being popular? Why? Why not?

Learn One day a man came to see Jesus. He was sick. He knew Jesus could help him. And Jesus did! The man was healed. He was happy. He told all his friends that Jesus made him well.

Everyone wanted to see Jesus. Jesus was very popular. But Jesus did not want to be popular. So He left town. He just wanted to please God. That was better than being popular.

Pray Dear Jesus, teach me that there are better things than being popular.

But more than anything else,
put God's work first and do what he wants.
Matthew 6:33

39

Caring for People

Mark 2:1–12

Think Have you ever had a friend break one of your toys?
Which did you care about more—your friend or your toy?

Learn One day many people went to a house to hear Jesus talk. They filled the whole house. A man who could not walk wanted to see Jesus too. He knew Jesus could make him well. But he could not get into the house. So his friends made a hole in the roof. Then they lowered the man down to Jesus.

Jesus was not angry that they made a hole in the roof. Jesus cared more about the man than about the house.

Pray Dear Jesus, help me to love people like You do.

Then you will live a life that honors the Lord, and you will always please him by doing good deeds.

Colossians 1:10

41

Loving the Unlovely

Matthew 9:9–13

Think Do you know some kids who do not have many friends?
Do *you* like them? Why? Why not?

Learn Matthew collected taxes. He would often take more money than he should. He did not have many friends. Not many people wanted to talk to him.

But Jesus asked Matthew to follow Him. Matthew h[ad] a party for Jesus. It was at his house. That made som[e] people mad. They did not think Jesus should go to Matthew's house. Jesus lov[ed] Matthew and wanted to b[e] his friend.

Pray Dear Jesus, help me to love people that even my friends do not like.

But don't forget to help others and to share your possessions with them. This too is like offering a sacrifice that pleases God.

Hebrews 13:16

Helping Others First

Luke 6:6–11

Think Do you like to help people? Why? Would you give up something you wanted to help them? Would you give up something you like to do to help a person? Why?

Learn It was the Lord's Day. Jesus saw a man with a hurt hand. The man wanted Jesus to make him well. The Jewish leaders did not think it was right to make someone well on the Lord's Day.

"Stretch out your hand," Jesus said to the man. The man stretched out his hand. Then Jesus made it well.

The Jewish leaders were mad at Jesus. But Jesus wanted to help the man. That was the right thing to do.

Pray Dear Jesus, bring someone into my life today I can help.

It is right to do good on the Sabbath.

Matthew 12:12

45

Asking for Help

Luke 6:12–16

Think When was the last time you were worried or scared?
What did you do?

Learn Jesus had to choose some close friends. The friends would be with Jesus for a long time. He would teach them many things. They would tell many people about Jesus.

Jesus prayed *all night*! He asked God to help Him choose the right friends.

God helped Jesus choose the right friends. When you have a hard job to do, do what Jesus did. Pray and ask God to help you. He will.

Pray Dear Jesus, help me to pray to You each night.

Everyone who asks will receive, everyone who searches will find, and the door will be opened for everyone who knocks.

Luke 11:10

Acting on Faith

Luke 7:1–10

Think Would you believe one of your friends if he or she told you something would happen? Why? Why not?

Learn A soldier had a servant who was sick. The soldier had heard about Jesus. He asked Jesus to make his servant well. Jesus started to go to the man's house.

But the man sent Jesus a message by some friends: "Just say the word, and my servant will get well."

The soldier believed in Jesus. He knew Jesus could heal his servant. All Jesus h to do was speak.

Pray Dear Jesus, help me to know that You will take care of me.

Faith that doesn't lead us to do good deeds
is all alone and dead!

James 2:17

Helping Those Who Hurt

Luke 7:11–17

Think When was the last time you felt sorry for someone?
What did you do to help?

Learn One day Jesus saw a woman leaving a city. The woman was crying. Her son had just died. The woman's husband was already dead. The woman was all alone.

Jesus looked at the woman. He felt sorry for her. "Don't cry!" Jesus said to her.

"Get up!" Jesus said to the dead boy. The boy sat up. He was alive! The woman did not cry anymore. Jesus made her happy again.

Pray Dear Jesus, help me to care for people like You do.

Children, you show love for others by truly helping them, and not merely by talking about it.

1 John 3:18

Accepting People Who Aren't Perfect

Luke 7:36–50

Think Do you know someone who is "different" from other kids?
Do your friends play with that person? Why? Why not?
Do you play with him or her? Why? Why not?

Learn Jesus went to eat at a friend's house. A woman came to see Him there. The woman had done wrong things. But she loved Jesus. She wanted Jesus to forgive her.

Jesus' friends did not think He should talk to her. They did not think she was a good person. But Jesus loved her. And Jesus forgave her. Jesus loves everyone.

Pray Dear Jesus, help me to love everyone.

Love comes from God, and when we love each other,
it shows that we have been given new life.

1 John 4:7

Being Part of God's Family

Luke 8:19–21

Think What do you like most about being in your family? Why?

What special things happen because you are in your family?

Learn One day Jesus was teaching people about God. Jesus' mother and brothers went to see Jesus. But there were many people. They could not see Jesus. So they sent Him a message.

"Your mother and brothers are standing outside," the message said.

But Jesus did not go out to see them. He said, "My mother and my brothers are those people who hear and obey God's message." That is us. We are part of Jesus' family!

Pray Dear Jesus, thank You for making me a part of Your family.

He loves us so much that he lets us be called his children, as we truly are.

1 John 3:1

Being Alone

Matthew 8:18, 24

Think Are you always busy doing things?
Are you ever too busy?
What do you do when you have too much to do?

Learn Jesus taught people about God. He made sick people well. Soon many people were going to see Jesus. But Jesus had to rest. He had to be alone.

So Jesus left the crowds. He went to the other side of the lake. He was so tired He slept in the boat.

When things get too busy for you, take time to get away.

Pray Dear Jesus, help me to know when to slow down.

But those who trust the LORD will find new strength.

Isaiah 40:31

Trusting God

Mark 4:35–41

Think When was the last time you were worried about something?
What did you do? Did you trust God to take care of your problem? Why? Why not?

Learn Jesus was tired. He told His friends, the disciples, to get in the boat. They were all going to the other side of the lake. Soon Jesus was asleep.

A storm came on the lake. Then water came in the boat. But Jesus still slept.

The disciples called to Jesus for help. He woke up. Jesus told the wind to stop blowing. The storm stopped.

Jesus took care of their problems. All they had to do was trust Him.

Pray Jesus, help me to come to You first when I have problems.

You, LORD God, are my protector.

Psalm 7:1

Believing in God

Luke 8:40–42, 49–56

Think Who do you turn to when you need help?
Are you sure you would get help? Why?
Has this person ever let you down?

Learn Jairus had one daughter. She was 12 years old. And she was dying. Jairus begged Jesus to come to his house. He knew Jesus could help his daughter.

Then a messenger came from Jairus's house. "Your daughter has died!" the person said.

Jesus told Jairus, "Don't worry! Have faith, and you daughter will get well."

Jesus went to Jairus's house. "Child, get up!" Jesu told her. The girl sat up. Jairus believed that Jesus could help his daughter. And He did.

Pray Help me to trust You more, Jesus.

The prayer of an innocent person is powerful, and it can help a lot.

James 5:16

Accepting Rejection

Luke 9:1–6

Think When did someone not want to play with you or be your friend?
How did you feel? What did you do?

Learn The disciples saw Jesus teach about God. Now it was their turn. Jesus sent them out to the towns. They were going to tell people about God too.

"If people won't welcome you," Jesus told them, "leave the town." Some people would not like the disciple Jesus did not want the disciples to be sad when people did not like them. Even Jesus was not liked b everyone.

Pray Dear Jesus, help me to act like You want me to act.

God blesses those people who are treated
badly for doing right. They belong to the kingdom
of heaven.

Matthew 5:10

Leaning on God

Mark 6:30–44

Think Do you try to solve problems by yourself? Or do you let someone else help you?

Learn People came to see Jesus. Soon there were 5,000 men and many women and children. The people became hungry. But the only food was one boy's lunch of five loaves of bread and two fish.

Jesus took the food. The He blessed it. The food fed all the people. There was even some left over! Jesus trusted in God. God took care of all those people.

Pray Dear Jesus, help me to know You will always take care of me.

With all your heart you must trust the LORD and not your own judgment.

Proverbs 3:5

Acting on Faith

Matthew 14:22–33

Think When your mom or dad picks you up, are you worried? Why? Why not?
Would you let someone you did not know pick you up? Why?

Learn The disciples were in a boat. They saw a man walking on the water. They thought it was a ghost. But it was Jesus.

So Peter got out of the boat. He walked on the water too. Then Peter got scared. And he started to sink.

Jesus pulled Peter out of the water. When Peter had faith in Jesus, he could walk on the water.

Pray Dear Jesus, help me to keep my eyes on You.

God can do anything.

Matthew 19:26

67

Being Clean on the Inside

Matthew 15:1–20

Think Do you wash your hands before you eat? Why?

How do you wash the inside of your heart?

Learn The Jewish leaders were mad. Jesus' disciples did not wash their hands when they ate. The Jews asked Jesus why His disciples did not follow this rule.

Jesus told them that wha[t] you eat does not make yo[u] clean or unclean. It is bad words you say that make you unclean. Your inside i[s] what hurts you.

Pray Dear Jesus, thank You for washing me on the inside. Help me to do the right things.

These commands are nearby and you know them by heart.
All you have to do is obey!

Sharing Glory with Others

Matthew 17:1–13

Think When was the last time you received credit for something you did?
Did you share that credit with others? Why? Why not?

Learn Jesus did not have to share His glory, but He did.

One day Jesus took Peter, James, and John with Him to a high mountain. Soon Jesus' clothes became white. His face started to shine like the sun. Then a bright cloud appeared.

A voice came out of the cloud. "This is my own dea Son, and I am pleased with him. Listen to what he says the voice said.

Jesus wanted His friends see that.

Pray Thank You for sharing Your glory with me, Jesus.

Love each other as brothers and sisters and honor others
more than you do yourself.

Romans 12:10

71

Serving Others

Mark 9:33–37

Think When have you argued with your friends about who is best?
Who won?
Is there a right way to become the best?

Learn One day the disciples took a walk. They had an argument. Each one wanted to be great. Each one wanted to be the best.

"What were you arguing about?" Jesus asked them. They did not tell Him.

He sat down with them. He told them that to be great, they must serve others.

Pray Jesus, give me a time today to serve someone else.

If you want the place of honor, you must become a slave and serve others!

Mark 9:35

73

Having Good Friends

Matthew 18:21–35

Think When was the last time someone asked you to forgive him or her?
What did you say?
Do you get tired of forgiving your friends?

Learn "How many times should I forgive someone?" Peter asked Jesus. Jesus told him a story.

A man owed the king a lot of money. He asked the king for forgiveness. The king forgave the man.

The man was happy.

Then he saw a friend. "Pay me what you owe!" he sai[d]

The man's friend asked forgiveness. But the man would not forgive him.

Jesus told Peter that we to forgive others with all hearts.

Pray Thank You for forgiving me, Jesus. Help me to forgive my friends too.

If you forgive others for the wrongs they do to you, your Father in heaven will forgive you.

Matthew 6:14

Deciding Who Is Important

John 6:60–69

Think What was the last thing you did that was hard?
Why did you do it?
Was it worth it? Why? Why not?

Learn People wanted to be with Jesus. But it was not easy. Jesus said some hard things. Many times people did not know what He meant.

Soon people started leaving Jesus. It was too hard to stay. Jesus turned t the disciples and asked if they wanted to leave Him too.

"There is no one else tha we can go to!" Peter said. "Your words give eternal life."

Pray Dear Jesus, I want to follow You. Help me to know what it means to be Your friend.

If any of you want to be my followers, you must forget about yourself. You must take up your cross and follow me.

Matthew 16:24

Forgiving, Not Punishing

John 8:1–11

Think When was the last time you did something wrong? Were you punished?
Were you ever not punished when you did something wrong? How did you feel?

Learn Some men brought a woman to Jesus. They said that she did a bad thing. Jesus stooped down as if He did not hear them. He wrote in the dirt.

Jesus stood up. "If any of you have never sinned, then go ahead and throw the first stone at her!" He said.

The men left. They had all done wrong. Jesus did not punish the woman. He forg her.

78

Pray Jesus, thank You for forgiving me when I do wrong.

Sin pays off with death. But God's gift is eternal life given
by Jesus Christ our Lord.

Romans 6:23

Giving Glory to God

John 9:1–34

Think Have you ever had a friend who said he or she did something you did?
What happened? How did it make you feel?

Learn One day Jesus saw a blind man. Jesus spat on the ground. Then He put the mud on the man's eyes.

"Go and wash off the mud," Jesus told him.

The man obeyed. Soon he came back. He could se Some people did not belie Jesus helped the man see.

But the man said, "I usec to be blind, but now I can see!" He knew God had made him see.

Pray You are so great, Jesus. I want people to know all You do for me.

We will always praise your glorious name. Let your glory be seen everywhere on earth.

Psalm 72:19

Taking Care of Others

John 10:1–21

Think When was the last time you helped a friend?
What did you do?
How does Jesus help you?

Learn Shepherds take care of sheep. They keep sheep safe. Shepherds make sure the sheep are fed. Sheep will die without shepherds.

Jesus is our shepherd. He keeps us safe. He feeds us and watches over us. The shepherd helps the sheep. Jesus helps us.

We can make sure our friends are all right. If they need help, we can help them. We can be like Jesus

Pray Dear Jesus, thank You for being the Good Shepherd. Show me how I can help others.

Since God loved us this much, we must love each other.

1 John 4:11

Letting Others in on the Fun

Luke 10:1–24

Think When was the last time you did something good for someone else? What were you doing? How did it make you feel?

Learn Jesus picked 72 friends. He had a big job for them to do. They would take His words to many towns.

They could heal those who were sick. And they could tell people about Jesus. Jesus let His friends do what He did. He did not want to be the only one doing good. He wanted His friends to help people too.

Pray Dear Jesus, help me to share good things with my friends.

Instruct them to do as many good deeds as they can and to help everyone.

1 Timothy 6:18

Helping Our Enemies

Luke 10:25–37

Think Who was the last person you helped? What did you do?
Have you ever helped someone who was not your friend? Why? Why not?

Learn One day Jesus told a story. Robbers beat up a Jewish man. Then they took his money. They left the man on the side of the road.

Two people walked by the man. But they did not help him. Samaritans did not like Jews. But a Samaritan stopp when he saw the man. He helped the Jewish man feel ter.

This is how we should ac We should even help peopl we do not like.

Pray Dear Jesus, I want to be more like the good Samaritan. And I want to be more like You.

Love your enemies, and be
good to everyone who hates you.
Luke 6:27

Making Jesus #1

Luke 10:38–42

Think Have you ever had more than two things to do at the same time?
What did you do? How did you decide what to do?

Learn Mary and Martha were sisters. They loved Jesus. One day Jesus ate at their house. Martha worked hard to fix a good meal. But Mary sat. She wanted to hear Jesus.

Martha was mad. "Tell her to come and help me!" she said.

"Mary has chosen what is best," Jesus said. She chose Jesus.

Jesus is the best. When we choose Him, we have done the right thing.

Pray Jesus, I choose You. I want You to be the most important thing in my life.

Love the Lord your God with all your heart,
soul, and mind.

Matthew 22:37

Asking God First

Luke 11:1–13

Think When you need help, who do you ask? Why

Learn Jesus' friends, the disciples, wanted Jesus to teach them how to pray. So Jesus told them a story.

A man went to his friend's house at midnight. He woke him up. Then he asked him for some bread.

"Don't bother me!" his friend said. But the man ke knocking. So his friend go up and gave him what he wanted.

Jesus told them to keep praying. God wants to giv you good things. He will answer your prayers if you keep asking Him.

Pray Dear Jesus, thank You for always giving me what I need.

I tell you to ask and you will receive, search and you will find, knock and the door will be opened for you.

Luke 11:9

91

Deciding Who to Follow

Luke 11:14–23

Think When was the last time you played a game with teams?

Whose team were you on? Could you have been on both sides? Why not?

Learn Jesus did great things. He helped a lot of people. And He healed many people. But some people did not believe in Jesus. They did not know He was the Son of God.

You cannot be for God and also against Him. Which side are you on?

Pray I want to be on Your side, Jesus. Help me to grow more like You.

If you are not on my side, you are against me.

Luke 11:23

93

Trusting God

Luke 12:13–34

Think When was the last time you worried? What did you worry about? Did worrying help?

Learn One day Jesus told a story about a rich man. He had no room for all his things. So he built a bigger place to keep all his things. Then he was happy.

But God said to him, "You fool! Tonight you will die. Then who will get wh you have stored up?"

Jesus did not worry abou collecting things on earth. He taught others about Go We should learn about Jesu not worry about things.

Pray   Dear Jesus, I do not want to worry about things. I want to think about You.

I tell you not to worry about your life. Don't worry about having something to eat, drink, or wear.

Matthew 6:25

95

Fearing No One

John 11:17–46

Think What are you afraid of? Why?
Do you think God can help you with your fear?

Learn Mary and Martha were sad. Their brother, Lazarus, was sick. They sent word to Jesus. But when He came, their brother was already dead.

Jesus said, "Your brother will live again!" Jesus went to the grave. "Come out!" Jesus said. Lazarus walked out of the grave! He was alive! There was nothing to fear. Even death could not defeat Jesus.

Pray Dear Jesus, help me not be afraid.

Everyone who has faith in me will live, even if they die.

John 11:25

97

Thanking God

Luke 17:11–19

Think What do you do when you receive a gift?
Why?
What do you do when God gives you something?

Learn Jesus was on His way to Jerusalem. He stopped at a village. He saw ten lepers, people who were very sick.

They called to Jesus, "Have pity on us!"

Jesus healed them. One of them came back to Jesus. He thanked Him for making him well. "Where are the other nine?" Jesus asked.

When God helps us, we should always thank Him.

Pray Dear Jesus, thank You for all You do for me.

It is wonderful to be grateful and to sing your praises.

Psalm 92:1

99

Not Giving Up on God

Luke 18:1–8

Think When was the last time you wanted something very, very much?
What did you do? What would you have done if your parents had said no?

Learn One day Jesus told this story. A widow was sad. She went to see a judge. She wanted him to help her. At first the judge would not help her. But she kept asking him.

Finally, the judge helped her. She asked him so much he was afraid she would wear him out. God will help us too. We just need to keep asking.

Pray Dear Jesus, help me to keep praying.

Never give up praying.

Colossians 4:2

Being Humble with God

Luke 18:9–14

Think Name some of your friends who are proud of themselves.
Why do they feel this way?

Learn Jesus told a story about two men. The two men went to pray. One man thanked God that he was not like other people. The man was proud of himself. The other man said, "God, have pity on me! I am suc[h] sinner."

Which man do you thin[k] made God happy? The se[c]ond man. God is not happ[y] when we are proud. He is happy when we are humb[le]

Pray Help me not to be proud, Jesus. Help me be humble.

If you put yourself above others, you will be put down. But if you humble yourself, you will be honored.

Luke 18:14

Loving Everyone

Luke 18:15–17

Think Have you ever felt as if no one loved you? Why?

Learn Jesus was busy. Many people came to see Him. One day parents came to see Jesus. They brought their children.

The disciples stopped them. They did not think Jesus had time to see children. But Jesus said, "Let the children come to me!"

Jesus loved all people, including children.

Pray Dear Jesus, help me to have time for every-one.

If you love each other, everyone will know that you
are my disciples.

John 13:35

Loving God Most

Luke 18:18–30

Think Who is your best friend? Why? What would you give up for that person? Why?

Learn A rich man spoke to Jesus one day. "What must I do to have eternal life?" he asked.

"You know the commandments," Jesus told him.

"I have obeyed all these commandments," the man said.

"There is one thing you still need to do," Jesus said. "Sell everything you own! Give the money to the poor."

The man walked away. He did not want to do that. So he gave up following Jesus.

106

Pray Dear Jesus, help me to always make You first in my life.

Come and be my follower.

Luke 18:22

107

Helping Others

Luke 19:1–10

Think When was the last time you helped someone?
What did you do?
How did it make you feel?

Learn Jesus passed through Jericho one day. Many people rushed to see Him. Zacchaeus wanted to see Him too. But he had a problem. He was short.

So he ran ahead of the crowd. He climbed a big tree. Then he could see Jesus too.

Jesus saw him. He knew Zacchaeus needed help. "Hurry down!" Jesus said to him. "I want to stay with you."

Jesus went to Zacchaeus's house. He helped Zacchaeus.

108

Pray Jesus, show me how I can help someone today.

Obey God's message! Don't fool yourselves by just listening to it.

James 1:22

Worshiping Jesus

John 12:1–8

Think How do you tell Jesus that you love Him? Do you go to church Sunday morning? What do you do there?

Learn One night Jesus was with Mary and Martha.

Mary took a bottle of perfume. It cost a lot of money. She poured the perfume on Jesus' feet. Then she wiped His feet with her hair!

Judas was mad. He wanted her to sell it and give the money to the poor.

"Leave her alone!" Jesus said. He knew she loved Him. That is why she did it. How do you tell Jesus that you love Him?

Pray I love You, Jesus. Help me to think about You in church.

You are worshiped by everyone! We all sing praises to you.

Psalm 66:4

Honoring Jesus as King

Matthew 21:1–11

Think What does a king do?
How do people act when they are near a king? Why?

Learn Jesus entered Jerusalem. It was a special visit.

He sat on a young donkey. The people spread their coats on the ground. The donkey walked over them. Some people cut branches off the trees. They waved them at Jesus.

They all shouted, "Hooray for the Son of David! God bless the one who comes in the name of the Lord."

They were cheering for their King. Jesus is the King

Pray You are my King, Jesus. Help me to be Your loyal follower.

I will praise you, my God and King, and always honor your name.

Psalm 145:1

Doing What God Wants

Luke 19:41–44

Think How do your parents feel when you disobey them? Why?
How do you think Jesus feels when we disobey Him?

Learn Jesus loved Jerusalem. It was God's city. Jesus wanted the people who lived there to obey God.

Jesus went to Jerusalem for the last time. He thought of how the people had not obeyed God. Jesus thought of how God would punish them.

Jesus was sad. He cried.

Pray Dear Jesus, help me not to make You sad.

Show me your paths and teach me to follow.
Psalm 25:4

Praying and Believing

Mark 11:12–14, 20–26

Think When was the last time God gave you or your parents something you prayed for?
When you pray for something, do you really believe God will give it to you? Why? Why not?

Learn Jesus and His disciples were hungry. Then they saw a fig tree. Jesus thought they could get something to eat. But the fig tree had only leaves on it. "Never again will anyone eat fruit from this tree!" Jesus said.

The next day the disciple saw the same tree. It was dried up. "Have faith in Go Jesus said.

When we believe in God great things can happen.

Pray I believe in You, Jesus. Help me to have more faith when I pray.

Everything you ask for in prayer will be yours,
if you only have faith.

Mark 11:24

Winning with Jesus

Mark 11:27–33

Think Do you know anyone who always wins?
Do you know anyone who tries to trick others?

Learn The Jewish leaders wanted to trick Jesus. "What right do you have to do these things? Who gave you this authority?" they asked.

Jesus was too smart for them. He asked them a question.

The leaders did not know how to answer. They were trapped!

"We don't know," they said to Jesus.

"Then I won't tell you who gave me the right to do what I do," Jesus said. Jesus always wins. When we follow Him, we win too.

118

Pray Thank You for letting me win with You, Jesus.

Thank God for letting our Lord Jesus Christ give
us the victory!
1 Corinthians 15:57

Giving All to Jesus

Mark 12:41–44

Think Do you give an offering at church? Why? Would you give an offering if you did not have much money? Why? Why not?

Learn Jesus and His disciples were talking. They stood by the temple. People came to give their offerings. One man gave a lot of money.

Then a woman came. She was poor. She gave her last few coins.

"This poor widow has put in more than all the others," Jesus said. He knew she gave everything she had.

God wants us to give from our hearts.

Pray Dear Jesus, what I have, I want to give to You.

Each of you must make up your own mind about how much to give.

Helping Jesus

Mark 14:12–16

Think What is the most special meal at your house? Thanksgiving? Christmas?
Who fixes the meal? Do you help?

Learn The Passover was a special meal. Jesus wanted to eat it with His disciples. He asked some of them to help Him. They got things ready for the meal. A man gave them a room to use.

You can help Jesus too. You can give money that will help a missionary tell about Jesus. You can give food to those who are hungry. When you help others, you help Jesus.

Pray Help me know what You want me to do, Jesus.

Whenever you did it for any of my people, no matter how unimportant they seemed, you did it for me.

Matthew 25:40

Letting God Pay People Back

Mark 14:17–21

Think Have you ever had a friend act mean to you? What happened?
Did you act mean back to him or her? Why?

Learn The disciples were Jesus' friends. He taught them many things. He loved them. Jesus knew one of them would do something mean to Him. He would turn Jesus over to His enemies.

Jesus told the disciples that one of them would betray Him.

They were very sad. "Surely you don't mean me!" each one said.

Jesus did not try to get even. He left that to God.

Pray Dear Jesus, help me to trust in Your fairness.

Don't try to get even. Let God take revenge.

Romans 12:19

125

Willing to Do Small Jobs

John 13:1–11

Think Would you do any job to help a friend? Or do you think some jobs are too small for you?

Learn Jesus and the disciples had walked a long way. Their feet were dirty. Often a servant washed feet. But Jesus washed the disciples' feet!

They did not understand. Jesus was the Son of God. Why should He wash their feet?

"You don't really know what I am doing," Jesus said, "but later you will understand."

Jesus was serving His friends. No job was too small for Jesus. Can any job be too small for us?

Pray Sometimes I think I am too big for small jobs. Help me remember that You washed dirty feet.

Anyone who can be trusted in little matters can also be trusted in important matters.

Luke 16:10

127

Forgetting Our Problems

Luke 22:14–23

Think Do you have the Lord's Supper at your church? What happens?
Why do people take the Lord's Supper? What do they think about?

Learn Jesus would have a long night. Then He would die.

Jesus had the Passover meal with His disciples first. He wanted them to remember what happened. He gave them the Lord's Supper. When they took it, Jesus told them to think about Him.

Jesus forgot His problems. He thought about the disciples. When we take the Lord's Supper we can forget our problems too. We can think about Jesus.

Pray Thank You, Jesus, for giving me a good way to remember You.

When you eat this bread and drink from this cup, you tell about his death until he comes.

1 Corinthians 11:26

Praying for Others

Luke 22:31–34

When was the last time you prayed for a friend?

Why did you pray for him or her? What happened?

Learn Jesus cared for the disciples. He loved them very much. Many times the Jewish leaders did not like what the disciples did. But Jesus stood up for them.

Jesus prayed for the disciples too. That was one of the best things Jesus did for them. He prayed a lot for a disciple named Peter.

"I have prayed that your faith will be strong," Jesus told him.

Do you want to help your friends? Pray for them.

Pray Dear Jesus, teach me how to pray for my friends like You prayed for Your friends.

Friends, please pray for us.
1 Thessalonians 5:25

Preparing Through Prayer

Luke 22:39–46

Think When was the last time you had to do something hard?
Did you worry about it? What did you do?

Learn Jesus did not want to die. What could He do? He prayed to God.

Jesus was so upset He started sweating. The sweat dropped from Him like blood. God did something special. He sent an angel to help Jesus.

Jesus prayed. And God helped Him. God will help us, too, if we ask Him.

Pray Sometimes I get scared when I have to do something hard. Jesus, help me to pray and ask You for help.

Father . . . do what you want, and not what I want.
Luke 22:42

133

Allowing God's Will to Be Done

John 18:1–11

Think Did your parents ever tell you to do something you did not like?
What was it? Did you do it?

Learn Jesus was with the disciples in the garden. Suddenly, a group of men came. They had weapons.

Peter took his sword. He was ready to fight. He cut an ear off one of the men.

"Put your sword away," Jesus said to Peter. He knew He must do what God wanted.

Jesus did not want them to fight. Jesus knew everything that happened to Him was part of God's plan.

134

Pray Dear Jesus, I want to obey You. I want to do what You want.

You are my God. Show me what you want me to do, and let your gentle Spirit lead me in the right path.

Psalm 143:10

135

Putting Everything in God's Hands

John 19:1–16

Think When was the last time your parents solved a problem for you? Why did you let them solve it? Would you let God solve a problem for you? Why? Why not?

Learn Jesus was brought to Pilate. Pilate was an important ruler. He told Jesus that he had the power to decide whether Jesus should die.

Jesus did not agree. He said, "If God had not given you the power, you couldn't do anything at all to me." Pilate was not in charge. God was in charge.

Pray Dear Jesus, I want You to be in charge of my life. Your way is best.

The world and the desires it causes are disappearing. But if we obey God, we will live forever.

1 John 2:17

Taking Our Place

Matthew 27:11–26

Think Has someone else ever been punished for something you did?
What happened? How did you feel?

Learn The crowd brought Jesus to Pilate. Pilate did not know what to do. He wanted to let Jesus go free. He could let someone in jail go free each year.

"Which prisoner do you want me to set free?" he asked the crowd.

"Barabbas!" they yelled. Barabbas had done many bad things. But Pilate set him free. Jesus died in his place. Jesus died in our place too.

Pray Dear Jesus, thank You for dying in my place. Thank You for taking my punishment.

The greatest way to show love for friends is to die for them.

John 15:13

139

Being Loving

Luke 23:26–38

Think Have people ever made fun of you? What did they say?

How did it make you feel? What did you do? What did you want to do?

Learn The crowd led Jesus out of the city. He was going to die. Many people were crying. They were very sad.

Some soldiers made fun of Jesus. "He should save himself," they shouted, "if he really is God's chosen Messiah!"

Jesus just prayed for ther "Father," Jesus said, "forgiv these people! They don't know what they're doing."

Do people make fun of you? Do what Jesus did. Pr Ask God to forgive them.

Pray Dear Jesus, help me to pray for people who make fun of me.

But I tell you to love your enemies and pray for anyone who mistreats you.

Matthew 5:44

Looking on the Inside

Luke 23:39–43

Think Can you tell what someone is like by looking at him or her? Why? Why not?
Have you ever been wrong about someone?

Learn Two men died with Jesus. They had done bad things. One of them made fun of Jesus. But the other man told him to be quiet.

"Remember me when you come into power!" the man said to Jesus.

"I promise that today you will be with me in paradise," Jesus told him.

Jesus looked past the man's outside. He saw what he was like on the inside.

Pray Dear Jesus, help me to look past the way people are on the outside. I want to see people on the inside.

Your words show what is in your hearts.

Luke 6:45

Helping Our Parents

John 19:25–27

Think When was the last time your parents helped you?

When was the last time you helped them?

How could you help them again?

Learn Jesus would die soon. His mother would be alone. Jesus saw her there at the cross.

John, one of the disciples, was there too. Jesus looked at His mother. "This man is now your son," Jesus said. Then He looked at John. "She is now your mother," He said.

That night Jesus' mother went to stay with John. Jesus never forgot His mother. Jesus took good care of her, even when He was on the cross.

Pray Jesus, thank You for giving me parents who care for me. Help me to know how I can help them.

Respect your father and your mother, and you will live a
long and successful life.

Deuteronomy 5:16

Keeping Our Promises

Luke 24:1–8

Think Have you ever broken a promise? Why? Do you think God breaks His promises? Why? Why not?

Learn Jesus told His friends that He would rise from the dead. But they forgot. Jesus was dead. They were sad.

In the morning some women visited the tomb. But the tomb was empty! Two angels stood next to them. "Jesus is not here! He has been raised from death," they told the women. They reminded th women of Jesus' promise t rise to life.

The women remembere Jesus had kept His promise

Pray Dear Jesus, thank You for keeping Your promises.

We must hold tightly to the hope that we say is ours. After all, we can trust the one who made the agreement with us.

Hebrews 10:23

Letting Jesus Teach Us

Luke 24:13–32

Think Do you know everything? If you have a question, whom do you ask? Why?

Learn Two men were walking on the road. It was right after Jesus died. They talked about what happened. Then Jesus appeared. He walked with them. But they did not know who He was.

"What were you talking about as you walked along?" Jesus asked them. They told Him what happened in Jerusalem.

"Why can't you understand?" Jesus said. Then He explained the Scriptures to them.

Pray Sometimes I have trouble understanding the Bible, Jesus. Please help me know what it means.

Teach me to follow, LORD, and lead me on the right path because of my enemies.

Psalm 27:11

Helping Others Learn

John 20:24–31

Think When was the last time you taught something to a friend? What did you do?
How did it make you feel? Why?

Learn The disciples knew Jesus was alive. They had seen Him. But one disciple, Thomas, had not seen Him and did not believe Jesus was alive. He wanted to see the nail scars.

A week later, the disciples were together once more. Thomas was with them. Jesus was there. Thomas saw Him.

"Stop doubting and have faith!" Jesus told Thomas. Jesus helped Thomas learn. We can help our friends learn too.

150

Pray Dear Jesus, help me to teach others when they do not understand.

Without faith no one can please God. We must believe that God is real and that he rewards everyone who searches for him.

Hebrews 11:6

Giving Our Friends Another Chance

John 21:15–19

Think When was the last time a friend did something to hurt you?
Did you forgive him or her? Did you trust the person again?

Learn Peter made Jesus sad. He told people that Jesus was not his friend. Peter knew he had done a bad thing. As soon as he did it, he cried.

Jesus was alive and with Peter again. Jesus did not get mad at Peter. Jesus asked Peter one thing, "Do you love me?"

Jesus had a big job for Peter. He wanted him to help others. He gave him a second chance. Peter went on to tell many people about Jesus.

Pray Dear Jesus, thank You for giving me a second chance. Help me to give my friends a second chance too.

Always be humble and gentle. Patiently put up with each other and love each other.

Ephesians 4:2

153

Sending Others to Help

Acts 1:1–8

Think Have you ever gotten help for someone? Why?

Could other people help better than you could? Why?

Learn It was time to say good-bye to Jesus. All the disciples were together. Jesus would soon leave. Then the disciples would be alone. Jesus knew they would need help.

"Wait here for the Father to give you the Holy Spirit," Jesus said. He had told them about the Holy Spirit. The Holy Spirit would help them.

154

Pray Father, thank You for sending the Holy Spirit. Help me to be willing to help others too.

Then I will ask the Father to send you the Holy Spirit who will help you and always be with you.

John 14:16

Telling Others About Jesus

Matthew 28:16–20

Think Have you ever told a friend about Jesus?
Why? Why not?
What did you say? What happened?

Learn Jesus taught the disciples many things. He taught them what to do. He taught them how to live.

It was time for Jesus to leave. But He had one more thing to tell them.

Jesus told them to go and make disciples. He said, "I will be with you always."

The disciples would not forget that. They would go many places. They would tell many people about Jesus. And Jesus would be with them.

156

Pray Thank You for always being with me, Jesus. Help me to tell someone about You this week.

Go and preach the good news to everyone in the world.

Mark 16:15

157

Helping Always

Mark 16:14–20

Think Are you a helper?
How do you help your friends?
Would it be possible for you to help all the time? Why?
Why not?

Learn It was time to say good-bye. Jesus told the disciples to tell everyone about Him. Jesus told them that the Holy Spirit would come soon.

Then Jesus was received up into heaven. He sat down at the right hand of God. But His job was not finished. He helps us every day. He never stops helping.

Pray Dear Jesus, thank You for helping me. I know You are watching over me.

Christ died and was raised to life, and now he is at God's right side, speaking to him for us.

Romans 8:34